Safety in the Kitchen

By Natasha Vizcarra
Illustrated by Giward Musa

Library For All Ltd.

Library For All is an Australian not for profit organisation with a mission to make knowledge accessible to all via an innovative digital library solution. Visit us at libraryforall.org

Safety in the Kitchen

This edition published 2022

Published by Library For All Ltd
Email: info@libraryforall.org
URL: libraryforall.org

Library For All gratefully acknowledges the contributions of all who made previous editions of this book possible.

This book was made possible by the generous support of Save The Children.

Save the Children

Original illustrations by Giward Musa

Safety in the Kitchen
Vizcarra, Natasha
ISBN: 978-1-922827-59-3
SKU02684

Safety in the Kitchen

The kitchen is full of delicious food and great smells.

But some things in the kitchen can hurt or harm us.

A hot stove can
burn you. Be careful!

A kettle or pot can
be too hot to touch.
Be careful!

Sharp knives can cut you. Be careful!

Bleach and house cleaning liquids are poisonous. Be careful!

Electric outlets can shock you. Be careful!

We need to be
careful to stay
safe in the kitchen.

You can use these questions to talk about this book with your family, friends and teachers.

What did you learn from this book?

Describe this book in one word. Funny? Scary? Colourful? Interesting?

How did this book make you feel when you finished reading it?

What was your favourite part of this book?

About the contributors

Library For All works with authors and illustrators from around the world to develop diverse, relevant, high quality stories for young readers. Visit libraryforall.org for the latest news on writers' workshop events, submission guidelines and other creative opportunities.

Did you enjoy this book?

We have hundreds more expertly curated original stories to choose from.

We work in partnership with authors, educators, cultural advisors, governments and NGOs to bring the joy of reading to children everywhere.

Did you know?

We create global impact in these fields by embracing the United Nations Sustainable Development Goals.

libraryforall.org

www.ingramcontent.com/pod-product-compliance
Lightning Source LLC
Chambersburg PA
CBHW040320050426
42452CB00018B/2944